BASHABI FRASER is a poet, edito
translator. She has lived in Koll
and now lives and writes in Edink
include *Ragas & Reels* (poems on migration and diaspora, 2012), *Scots Beneath the Banyan Tree: Stories from Bengal* (2012), *From the Ganga to the Tay* (an epic poem, 2009), *Bengal Partition Stories: An Unclosed Chapter* (2006; 2008), *A Meeting of Two Minds: The Geddes Tagore Letters* (2005) and *Tartan & Turban* (poetry collection, 2004). Bashabi has been widely anthologised as a poet. Her awards include the 2015 Outstanding Woman of Scotland awarded by Saltire Society, Women Empowered: Arts and Culture Award and the IAS Prize for Literary Services in Scotland. In addition to being a member of Scottish Pen, and serving on their executive committee for two terms, Bashabi is also a Patron of the Federation of Writers in Scotland and an executive committee member on the Writers in Prison Committee (Scotland) and the Poetry Association of Scotland. She is a Trustee of the Kolkata Scottish Heritage Trust, and is a Director on the Board of the Patrick Geddes Memorial Trust and is on the Management Committee of the Scottish Association of Writers. With a PhD in English, Bashabi is a Professor of English and Creative Writing and cofounder and Director of the Scottish Centre of Tagore Studies (ScoTs) at Edinburgh Napier University and a Royal Literary Fund Fellow based at Queen Margaret University, Edinburgh. Bashabi is also an Honorary Fellow at the Centre for South Asian Studies at the University of Edinburgh.

Letters to My Mother and Other Mothers

BASHABI FRASER

Luath Press Limited
EDINBURGH
www.luath.co.uk

To Ma and all the women
who have lit our lives with their
warm protective flame.

First published 2015

ISBN: 978-1-910745-14-4

The paper used in this book is recyclable. It is made from low chlorine pulps produced in a low energy, low emissions manner from renewable forests.

Printed and bound by
Bell & Bain Ltd., Glasgow

Typeset in 10.5 point Sabon by
3btype.com

Contents

Acknowledgements

I am grateful to the following anthologies in which some of the poems in this collection have been published: *Café Dissensus*, Issue 5, January 2014 (available at www.cafedissensus.com/2014/01/01/poem-mariam/); Platinum Jubilee Commemoration Volume, *Gokhale Memorial Girls College* (Kolkata: New Rainbow Lamination, 2014); *Bharatiya Engraj Kobita*, eds, Somdatta Mandal and Soma Mukherjee, (Kolkata: Abhijan Publishers, 2012), a bilingual poetry anthology; *Lion's Milk*, eds, Alan Riach and Ian Brown. (Glasgow: Kennedy and Boyd, 2012), a bilingual poetry anthology. *Temba Tupu!* (*Walking Naked*): *African Women's Self-Portrait*, ed, Nagueyalti Warren (Trenton, NJ and Asmara, Eritrea: African World Press, 2008); *Freedom Spring: Ten Years On*, eds, Suhayl Saadi and Catherine McInterney (commissioned by Glasgow City Council, 2005) and BBC Scotland.

Introduction

I REMEMBER holding my mother's hand and being taken to a school where I did not write a word in the admission test, but was put into a class with kids two years older than I was because I impressed the head teacher with my chatter. When the results came out at the end of the year, I skipped gleefully to my mother and told her that the teacher had said I had come second. My mother discovered from the report that I had actually come second last. She was amused, but did not say anything to dishearten me. In fact, when some years later I found the Indian system baffling after my London years (1960–63), and didn't do well in the first term exams, she looked sad, but once again, did not reprimand me. I think that was what spurred me on to try and discover my potential, which I read in her discerning eyes that seemed to have every faith in my ability. I don't think I failed, after that, to fulfil my mother's expectations in me.

As a child, I was a poor eater and I remember her patience on the ship that took us from Bombay to Marseille, as I never finished a meal and always assured her that I would eat various items of food 'later'. She knew my game and played along with it, piling continental pears and brownies on our cabin table which I carried from the dining room and blissfully forgot. One of the earliest memories of my mother is of her pouring cornflakes into my breakfast bowl and sitting with me at the table, a soft smile on her lips as she listened intently to me as I got ready to go to school on cold winter days in London. And that is how she remained, a quiet, gentle presence, enjoying conversations around her, a listener rather than a raconteur.

She came from a generation of Bengali women who found themselves displaced by the Indian Partition. Her family had to leave all their property behind. She was one of eight sisters and one brother, and her doctor father sent them to a boarding school as her mother had died when she was quite small. My grandfather believed that education was the only wealth that could give his daughters security when they found they had lost everything to a mindless political border. My mother was a working woman as all my maternal aunts were (apart from my eldest aunt), and like many post-Partition Bengali women, they joined the band of breadwinners for struggling families.

I soon realised that my mother was quite special. She was the only lady lecturer in her department at her college where she taught in Kolkata before we went to London. She won a scholarship to the London School of Economics where she did a Research Masters. She was the first woman lecturer at the university where she taught when she came back to India, the first lady to become a Reader in Geography and the first woman Professor in the subject. She was a determined lifelong learner. She decided to learn Hindi by speaking to our cleaning lady from Bihar in Hindi. Her initial attempt was a hilarious, Bengalicised Hindi which made her employee smile and say, '*Maaji*, you can say it in Bangla.' But my mother persevered in spite of our giggles and succeeded in speaking fluent Hindi at the end of the day.

She told me that she had been hopeless at needlework at school and I was quite envious of my friends whose mothers were expert dressmakers. My mother did her best to buy me tastefully chosen dresses, or discovered deft tailors in the labyrinthine alleys of a backward city, and let me design my clothes, for which she was willing to scour fabric shops to get the right material. I think she never forgave herself for her lack of dressmaking skills. Well into her middle age, her sewing teacher acted as a private tutor and after that she made our curtains, our quilt and cushion covers, my nightdresses, her sari blouses, my father's pyjamas and finally, some of my dresses. She was neat and her eye for perfection is evident in a couple of knitted jumpers I have retained.

My father loved my mother's singing voice. She could play the harmonium from the time she was three and could accompany any music, playing along as she heard the notes unfold. Later on, she was able to coax her favourite tunes from my daughter's piano. I once witnessed her tentatively approaching the strings of a violin and was startled to hear her play a scale slowly and then put the instrument down with embarrassment when she knew she had an audience. She had a sensitive ear for music and could play by ear. I remember her playing to a Russian song once when we had a visitor who sang at our request. I spent my holidays on the university campus where my parents taught and we always put up concerts, dance dramas and plays when we came home for holidays. It was possible to do this as my mother was willing to come back from a day's teaching and sit with us through rehearsals every day for a month or so, playing the harmonium and leading the singing. She had a great sense of rhythm, which was ideal for our dances. Yet she was not trained. So, again in her middle age, she had a private tutor to help her to understand ragas, and after that one year of training, she never failed to recognise a raga or a *mishraraga* (a creative combination of ragas).

My mother was the founder secretary of the University's Ladies Club; she started the Ladies Club

Mela, an art competition, and pioneered a library for children, a classical dance class and a singing class for us and a sewing class for the ladies. She had started writing and directing plays when she was an undergraduate and continued to do so when she was teaching, and both the Ladies Club and the university campus children acted her plays and performed under her direction. The plays embodied her infectious sense of humour and dwelt on social issues related to women. She encouraged me to train in classical Indian dance and develop a parallel semi-professional dance career. This training has shaped the rhythmic patterns of my poetry.

She was an all-rounder. At Scottish Church College where she studied, she was a badminton blue. I always found this difficult to believe as she was the slowest walker on the campus. I used to tease her and say that from a distance I couldn't decide whether she was moving forward or backward, which always made her smile. But once I played a badminton match against her and witnessed her calculating skills. She stood in one place and made me run around as she alternately sent the shuttle cock to the back of the court or gently slipped it over the net, resulting in me missing it several times. She proved to be a formidable contestant. Needless to say, I lost each set I played with her. She was great with numbers and I took my Maths homework to her always. She never failed me. Her sharpness and the ease with which she did long calculations in her head always amazed us. I did not inherit her ability with Maths.

She was entrepreneurial, innovative and enterprising. When we came to the university campus in the wilderness of the Himalayan foothills from London, my mother found that her 'furnished quarters' consisted of a bucket with a rope to fetch water from a well and a kerosene lantern, as there was no electricity or running water. She was intrepid. She was a creator and created beauty around her. We had some of the most beautiful murals on walls that she had painted in our university quarters. She had truckloads of alluvium delivered to replace her stony top soil in her garden, on which she worked with my father and aunt who lived with us. She coaxed a garden out of the once stony soil, which became proverbial for its abundance of many-hued flowers and some of the sweetest mangoes and guavas on the campus.

Yet she remained a dedicated researcher and published academic articles and books and enjoyed teaching in spite of her many-faceted activities. She was a staunch defender of her students against bureaucratic regulations. She never forgot the indignity inflicted on refugees as a result of Partition and secretly helped many domestic hands to find ways to become financially viable. In fact, she hated the social reality of an underclass and did all within her limited means to help every maid, gardener, and cleaner in her employ to become self-sufficient.

The violence of the 1940s made my mother an unswerving believer in the efficacy of non-violence, and she encouraged the education of girls and women as the way forward for nation building. I guess this is what has made me – her investment in my education, her Gandhian approach to social problems, her Tagorean creativity and her feminine will. She loved poetry. She and my father were loyalists who were the first to listen to every poem I wrote and formed my private cheer group, which kept me devoted to poetry on the one hand, and allowed a pile of bad verse to accumulate on the other. When I won my first poetry prize in London as a seven-year-old – the Commonwealth Scholar Prize

– my mother, with my father, walked on air. As far as my mother was concerned, being a poet was the best role one could have in the world.

I could speak to my mother about everything – social injustice, climate change, women's rights, music, plays, films, politics, books, my crushes, my friends' romantic escapades... So when she lost her short-term memory and receded into her world of near silence as a result of multiple minor strokes that led to acute dementia, I lost my defender and my patient listener. My mother died in 2005. For a long time I could not write about her, though there was so much to write. Then one night I dreamt of her, not as she had been in her post-twilight years, but as she was, the gentle, patient, generous, encouraging, liberal and strong woman that I knew and the first poem in this collection wrote itself. Since then, the 'letters' have flowed as a conversation that would have flowed with my mother, as I would have shared my thoughts – both personal and on world events – with her.

The sequence to 'Other Mothers' is a natural stream that flows in the same strain. Two poems for young couples were requested by their mothers to be read at their weddings. This final section embodies my mother's feminine will and her concern about feminine potential being threatened by deep despondency or thwarted by death. The poems pose the questions she would have raised or asked about the lives of women and their children – in whom she would have found a deep interest – a human interest that perhaps draws all our nurturing, creative mothers together in one magic circle.

Bashabi Fraser

Letters to my Mother

I saw you last night

I saw you as you were, last night
I had brought a friend home
I hadn't warned you
You opened the door
Your face was soft as it always was
Suffused by the magic of twilight
The open door let in.
I said, Ma, this is my colleague
You smiled, your eyes a melting caress
You stepped back to let us in
Your dining table was laid, expectant
Behind you. You walked effortlessly
To the kitchen to bring in an extra plate
Your quiet acceptance flowed
From your inherent generosity
Before unannounced strokes
Froze sections of your once discerning brain
And you altered to the unquestioning presence
That wasn't and yet was you,
But I saw you last night
Not as you had become in the post-twilight years
But as you always were
And will be for me, my mother.

The things you did for us

You could open windows
And let the slow dawn sneak in
You could coax the jasmine to bloom beyond its season
You could have rooms dusted, meals cooked
Floors swept and vases stacked
Putting order to a home you had rocked
To sleep the night before
Waking now to your sweet song
And the rhythm of your chores.
You could tend the mango tree to tender sweetness
You could urge guavas and lemons to abundance
You could fill the lonely evening with Iman ragas
You could drench the parched earth with the vigour
Of your giving spirit that curled around our days
And gathered us in the folds of your embrace.

I will remember you

Whenever I see one sturdy soul
Giving up comforts and career
To teach children in unmapped spots
I can feel your spirit near.

Whenever I see a door open
To a beggar, and watch a woman
Pour grain and money, offer a sari
I see you once again.

Whenever I am on a train watching
Vendors with trinkets, snacks or tea
Urging their wares on commuters wearily,
I can see you buying from each one tirelessly.

Whenever the nearby village drunk
In desperate hunger looks for work
I see you finding tasks for him
In your neat garden, for a week.

Whenever maids are driven out
On charges of unproven crime
I see you giving them a place
Of dignity in your own home.

Whenever there is a lamp to light
A pain to ease, a scar to heal
Whenever there is a thirst to quench
I see your spirit revealed.

If I could bring you back

I wish I could bring you back again
And turn the table round this time
I'd bring you tea in bed my mother
I'd open curtains for the sun to shine
On your soft features in your prime.
I'd comb your hair and plait it neatly
I'd fold your clothes upon a chair
I'd check the water was warm and plenty
For you to have your morning shower
I'd have the breakfast laid and ready
With marmalade, toast and Darjeeling tea
I'd pack your lunch with imagination
Just as you had done for me.
And when you came home, hungry and tired
I'd wash your weariness away
I'd lay out a feast fit for a queen
And then I'd let your sore head lie
On my lap for me to ease
Till your eyelids knew the solace
Of comfort born of love and peace
And I'd be grateful that all day
I'd kept all hurtful words away
That I had not in selfish pleasure
Forgotten your waiting self
Watching through the waking hours
For me to come back well and safe
But have the knowledge that like you
I was undemanding and true
To you, my mother.

The boy from Chittagong

You loved the shy boy from Chittagong
With his halo of dark curls
His easy blush, and alert brain
His meagre pockets awoke the mother in you
You found joy in buying his meals
And you watched him eat with satisfaction
Though you too were an underfed student.
Your doctor's family was not good enough
For his Brahmin background
And because you had married for love
It was a good excuse to overlook the need
For a celebratory wedding.
There were no gold bangles for your giving hands
No delicate necklace to ornament the throat
That could fashion intricate melodies
No-one blessed you with crockery to grace your table
Saris to heighten your dignity
Or a bed to bless your future with their son.
The conch shell that could have sent
An auspicious note to prophesy a bountiful future
Was silent and no lamp was held
To behold and welcome your soft face and doe eyes.
All your life Ma, you gave – meals, puja clothes,
Wedding gifts, unbounded hospitality –
Yet all your life you did not expect any return
Or recognition of your countless acts of love,
For you had married for love, exercised your choice,
And though you had a position the world revered
It was only reluctantly accepted by those whose
Lives you watched with your protective concern.

Thundering hooves

You watched the clouds' courtship of intent –
Supplicants of an importunate river
Into which the sun bled in a quiver
Of streaks as it suspended its departure.
You stood beside your friend
Your *archals* free like larks' wings.
You were lulled by the stormy serenade
Unaware of the threatening hooves behind you
Of bulls in action, hurtling down the slope.
But he had seen the dust cloud vault
As he stood behind you, too shocked to shout.
He intervened, butting you both in a catapult
That troubled you and your startled friend
Out of the pair's path at their journey's end.

The flower thieves

It was that in-between moment
When a tentative darkness hovered
Poised to catch the first overture
Of light pushing the frontiers.

You sat silently on a cane *mora* on your veranda
Watching the furtive shadows
Drift into your nurtured garden
To pluck the fruits of your passion for their puja.

You startled them, saying leave some
On the bushes and be gentle when
You pick them. They were interrupted
In their theft, picked hurriedly and left

Leaving you smiling at the fair remnants
They conceded to save for the symphony of dawn.

The hesitant flowers

There is something I don't understand Ma
One September I planted bulbs while the sun
Lingered like a lazy lout in a bed
Waiting to be made for the next visitor
Who had arrived and raged inwardly in the lounge.
I had chosen the bed carefully,
Separating the bluebells and the snowdrops
From the daffodils, narcissi and tulips
Plunging each bell jar of latent life
Into groves that would prove productive,
Ensuring a succession of colour from silvery January
Through multicoloured February
To golden March and butterfly resplendence
In April and May, knowing that
All the time the bluebells would stay
In their sequestered shade, away
From the beds under the sun spilled day.
But an unknown presence has breathed
On their sleeping dreams and though they
Have stretched and lifted their green feelers
To wake and wonder, they have not
Yet distinguished themselves in a flourish
Of rainbow festivity with the wish of plenty
That I had invested in their planting
One September, when I planned with hope.

In London where you were

Your granddaughter is now a Londoner
Just as you were half a century ago, my Ma
And we are with her on a very cold February
Morning, when the sun is warm but not robust
Enough to melt the shards of ice that float
On puddles beside the kerb of terraced rows
Of an endless curve of houses, one of which holds
The one person you held so dear that she could
Do no wrong in your eyes, then or now or ever.
We are waiting Ma, for one significant call
From the hospital, announcing one empty bed
Ready to receive your little angel who will
Then enter the labyrinthine depths where we
Cannot accompany her, but maybe you
Will meet her there Ma, and put her head
In your capacious lap and tell her stories
While the surgeon's knife investigates and knowing fingers
Insert the tubes that bypass her clogged
Arteries. You can sing the blood flow into
Her blocked legs and smooth her future days
As you stroke back her furrows and hair
And present her a beautifully packed
Gift, renewed, replenished and ready to shine
In a world where you once watched her uncurl
Her petals under your tender admiration –
My mother.

St George's Hospital

She was as you would not have liked to have seen her
A body, with the soul smothered in protected sleep
Numerous tubes marking her territory in
Invasive roads, mapping and claiming her frame.
She jerked awake intermittently, and seeing us
Sitting there, willed her eyes to open wide
In a wondrous dreamy effort to stay alert
For seconds, till her morphine-induced drowsiness
Forced her eyelids close – invisible fingers pulling
Her back to a world only you could enter with her.
One morning, her furrowed forehead
Outlined her nagging fear. 'Where is all the blood going?'
Was her first question, as she watched
The transfusion tube dripping red like the Central Line –
Into her supine wrist – someone's donation
Now pulsing her to recovery, monitored
By your unseen presence.

The speeding car

When a speeding car threw up your
Granddaughter, like a tennis racket
Sending a ball over the net, she
Landed unconscious, with no indication

Of bouncing back. But you were
Watching, urging her breath back
Letting her concussion crack open
The clot that was to set her free.

With her dancer's legs frozen with pain
As her blood stopped its replenishing
Journey, you oversaw the tests
That detected the claudication

You waited and supervised the bypassing
Miracle that set her limbs free.

The planned journey

after your granddaughter's accident

The journey was planned in time and space Ma;
Trusting the meticulous two-minute succession
Of tubes in London, I arrived at Balham
To move to Croydon by the overground train
To catch the Gatwick connection in time
For the take off. The queue was unmoving,
The counter slow as impatience and passengers grew,
I watched oyster card holders ease through
The barriers, envying their ability to forge ahead –
When a voice on the tannoy jerkily said
'Passengers on platforms one and two
Please leave the station now.'
The lucky divers surged back carrying
In their high tide a ripped string
Of an attendant, rippling with terror
As she wailed 'he jumped in front of me.'

A confluence

I was back at the Nehru Centre
This time with my dialogue between rivers
That started their philosophical reverie
Six years ago, when you were sentient.
Your knowledge had the breadth of the Ganga
Your serenity in the face of my frustration, mirrored
The pragmatic calm of Tay on reflective days.
Your comments stirred the depths of turgid currents
And probed and provoked every night
Till the journey could find its own legitimate end
Even when your mind withdrew and your light faded –
The dialogue has continued like two timeless streams
As your granddaughter picked up the tone
Of her Scottish comfort zone, and gave voice
To Tay's meditative volubility –
Reaching out to my impression
Of Ganga's impetuosity
In a confluence you would be endorsed
By the vision that you have passed on.

A presence in absence

It was warm Ma, when I left Kolkata
It was 4° the night I arrived in Edinburgh
I left Baba with moist eyes and a longing, lingering look
I met Neil with his delighted smile and sense of relief
In every room in Kolkata, you looked down on me
At every door in Edinburgh, I felt your absence
I tasted your sophisticated artistry in every meal there
I missed the intimacy of affectionate offering at my table here
The gardens had the green sheen of your magic touch there
While here our grass is sheeted under the silence of snowy fingers
Kolkata was troubled with the pressure of its millions
While Edinburgh streets were muffled and deserted
But this time Ma, the Boi Mela[1] saw a confluence
As the Scottish Pavilion took centre stage
And Scots made the headlines and mingled with the city
The ghosts in the Scots Cemetery woke up and waltzed
In the corner that is forever Scotland
For the tropical grass has been cut back
To give them a dance floor as they celebrate life on the Hugli
The restoration of their gravestones in a renewal
Of a shared history, which flows like a tide
Between a tale of two cities unfolding
As I journey back and forth
From your spiritual hearth
To the bracing north
Carrying your presence in my very breath
My mother.

1 Book Fair – a reference to the Kolkata Book Fair in 2009 when Scotland was the Theme Country.

Frozen frolic

This year Ma, the icebergs melted
And the warm Gulf Stream was overpowered by a
relentless
Current of frozen frolic that cavorted
Across the Atlantic and sent chilling clouds
To muffle our December nights.
After three decades, we woke to
The certainty of a white Christmas
That you encountered in '60s London
Your granddaughter built a snow meercat
Beside our bird table, surprising the blackbird
That inspected its button eyes with beady attention.
The canal froze, leaving the coupling swans
To waddle in middle-aged portliness
Having lost the grace of propelling waters
The sole bachelor goose that followed
The brood each hatching cygnet spring
Was a clownish uncle, cheering the silent duo
With his skating antics
As he slid with abandon
While the working world stood still.
The walkers revelled
On the banks of a waterway
They knew was still there
Just as the feathered populace knew,
Waiting to flow free once again
When the mica surface splintered
With the Gulf Stream's forgiving return.

An Icelandic Saga: Part 1

Long years ago, while I played on the ship
You walked down the gangway to Pompeii
To witness the silencing of a whole civilisation
Under the determined flow of an insidious stream.
But this time it wasn't Vesuvius that belched
But an angry fist of fiery cloud
That billowed out from the faultline of icy stolidity
In a country that knew the coldness of total collapse.
As the world abandoned this resting place for Thor
A message from the earth's heaving centre
Was sent out in scattered ash and raving silicon
A reminder of death that hovers or looms.

There was one image of that smothered city
That you would never forget, of a mother
Clutching her babe, immortalised by that remorseless
stream
Which did not churn out this time, content to see the
unseen for now.

An Icelandic Saga: Part II

The people lost the battle and the fifth terminal
Was built at Heathrow. It was there
Where your husband sat and counted three planes
Flying every five minutes. Your calculator brain
Would have added them in seconds for each day,
For every week, and month and year
Planes that houses round the runways
Have heard soaring off and zooming in
Ever since they can remember,
Like the rain – a reliable reality,
More than the sun. But a week ago
They woke up to a strange new dawn
Of bird-song, which the small winged race
Set up in full-throated ease to fill a sky
Empty, blue and utterly free.

Climate refugees

We went to see a film on Climate Refugees
Where I felt your presence in the audience
Approving of the director's epiphanic images
Of the disastrous effect of depleting forests,
The unrestrained harnessing of rivers,
The traffic-choked roads, the thoughtless smoke
Of industries, the laying bare of grassland
Jeopardising multitudinous animal flocks
The bartering of prime land for building work.

You would have felt the weariness of women
Walking desert miles to fetch pitchers of water
Your eyes would have caressed the children
Leaving play to queue up for food aid gifts.

But even you Ma, could not have foreseen
How close to the brink we stand of new Continental shifts
As the Sunderbans will disappear with their millions,
The Maldives will dive below the Indian Ocean
Tuvalu will sink without a blink
From the world's nations, and islands
Of the East and West Indies, which drew
The traders and colonisers in a struggle for ownership,
Will not have any competitor vying for their crew
As these tropical dreams are engulfed by mighty streams.

The rivers you knew, flowing with majestic assurance
From the Himalayan peaks and Tibet's proud plateau –
The Ganga and the Jamuna, the Mekong and the Irrawaddy
The Yangsi Kiang, now flood in spring
And shrink every year, as the snow melts steadily
Without replenishment as the global warming continues
With the debate many spurn –
Not ready to accept the climate refugees
Marooned to greet a churning grave.
So the earth is stoically poised now
For a new embrace Ma,
Bracing itself for a salt-water invasion
That will substantially deplete its population.

As Europe debates Turkey's entry

We cannot curb the spiralling hate
While we debate Turkey's fate
And remain guards at Europe's gate.
A 'Christian Club' can open doors
And set the table for past foes
And all can sit down to shared meals
In an open world with open deals.
Then the mists of doubt will rise
And lift the clouds that darken skies
To soften Iraq's groaning cries.
And my daughter can walk free
From doubts about identity
A member of humanity
As powers do not invade
And new promises of trade
Create a world where borders fade.

Japan's triple jeopardy

First there were the tremors
Which rippled across the surface
Then they turned to a feverish
Violence that shook tethered lives.
It was as if a gigantic serpent
Had woken from its centurian sleep
And was uncoiling and rising
To splinter its subterranean hold.

Then came the wave, like a mighty
Hooded cobra, dark in intent
Fresh from Neptune's grasp
It swept through city streets
And somnolent car parks
Gathering buildings and vehicles
Like toy pieces that a greedy
Boy grabbed and scattered with abandon
And then, Ma, came the chilling fear
As nuclear reactors in sealed holders
Were tested beyond human expectation
And Japan which has been at peace
For over six decades, awoke to the reality
Of radioactive waves slithering through
Her population who had believed the ghosts
Of Hiroshima and Nagasaki would not return.

The British barricade of snow

Do you remember when the pipes froze in London
And we ran round with kettles
Like little Jacks and Jills enjoying
A make believe fun game
Looking for wells to send down pails
While our snowman kept vigil
On dark winter afternoons
His beady eyes watchful,
His smile a fixed freeze?

The snowflakes came this November
Impatient and determined like men with a purpose
They draped the sky with intent
They stretched like an army
They laid every city in an unflagging siege
They charged their ammunition in a volley of cloud flakes
They drifted like eiderdown from thousands of bombers
That shred their prize cargo before sprinkling their targets
Which were totally unaware of this unanticipated
Invasion from the chilled ocean's breast.

It was a one-sided war-game
Met without resistance, as an unprepared
Nation turned indoors to wait
For the melt down and floods that would
Mark a reprieve in a temporary truce.

Nero's Guests

When Nero knew that Rome was burning
He was afraid. He called the great and the mighty –
Romans all – to a feast they would never forget
They were indulged with delicacies that were delectable
But how did Nero keep those feast fires burning?
Every time a new dish needed fuel, his prisoners fanned
  the flames
A convict or a slave – the dispossessed and condemned
Were fed into the fire to keep it alight
To feast the Romans, his guests honoured with human
  flesh.
So Nero's guests were the privileged survivors
And this is the story that was recalled
Ma, to describe a rich world of compensation paid
  farmers
Who were paid to produce less, to lead another half
Of growers who feel the tug of their hollow stomachs.
They can only watch their lustreless children, their
  despairing wives
Whose fires are unlit, witness their crops unsold
Their harvest discarded by a market economy
That drives them to suicide, in alarming droves
To feed the fires of a closely guarded first world
Of rich nations – Nero's guests today
Who feast while a raging fire burns the rest to ashes.

Camp Hope

Two thousand feet below the rock surface of the earth
Dug up walls caved in, creating what might have been
A living grave for thirty-three miners trapped
In Chile's copper mine, where safety measures
Were not an issue before this unwonted accident, Ma.
Seventeen days of uncertainty strained
The entombed men's hopes and their families'
Till one narrow shaft reached them to send
Upwards to the world of the living
The message with the image that ascertained
They were all alive! So the world watched
With bated breath, as Chile's President
Decreed that they would be hauled back to their midst
in time
Under pressure of thirty-three families
Those families who set up tents in what became known
as Camp Hope
That signal of stoicism in eternal watchmen
Was realised as schools opened petals, health centres
breathed
New life and the world watched their determination.
A capsule cage was created for freedom's cause
The metal shaft was widened to slide the cage through
The lifeline to the thirty-three subterranean captives
And the rocket, once ready, did not soar
But dived below, journeying after sixty-nine days,
Making thirty-three trips and six more
To bring back the trapped from earth's bowels

To the sunlight and breeze and their families –
With the engineers, the doctor and technicians
Who followed them to the nether world and back
As the world watched with credulity
And the thirty-three families wept with relief
And a thousand stars applauded
A new set of heroes who had found
That lives are precious to families who hold a nation
And the world to account to kindle hope
And keep the Olympian torch of life burning.

Liu Xiaobo

Do you remember, Ma, watching a revolution
When *World This Week* let us witness
A vigil lit with hope
As students camped in Tiananmen Square?
But they could not move the state machine
To listen to the voice of a generation
Wishing change. Liu Xiaobo moved in
To urge them to leave, but the voice of reason
Could not stop them or the tanks that rolled in.

From then, this sole soldier in love
With the freedom true words can bring
Has fought his lone battle,
Hidden from his people, but heard
The world over at the wind speed of wings
Of doves with a message of peace
That has moved from Jingzhou Prison to Oslo
Where an empty chair marked the presence
In absence of a man who cannot be silenced
For now or forever.

Arab Spring

They call it the Arab Spring Ma,
A new beginning –
But is it? Has that sense of freedom
Of a people who traded with kingdoms
On either side of their middle kingdom
Not always existed?

They brought the east and west together
As goods and words crossed borders
Their steeds and boats defied the weather
They were the Sindbads, not marauders

But repressive regimes aided by weapons
Sold by powerful and developed nations
Have constrained their enterprise for a while
While their oil left their soil to nurture lifestyles
That they could only dream of through decades
Till one young fruit vendor in the market street
Who struggled with bribes that he had to meet
To earn a few dollars in corruption's arcades
Found his pride manhandled by a government official
And his dreams of his sisters attending university
Were shattered on that crucial
Day, when Mohamed Bouazzi angered a city
As he set himself aflame,
The oil that he could not burn
In a country that has no oil
The money that he could not earn
Had lit that dignity to shame

His oppressors, his act became a foil
For other nations as a chain reaction followed
From the dusty streets of Sidi Bouzid
That spread from an outraged population
A battle cry that rang beyond Tunisia's masjids
For freedom that has seen this uprising
Ma, of a dormant and dignified Arab Spring.

Arab women

Perceptions of the hijab
Have now been challenged Ma
By women who led picketing crowds
Across the Arab world. They unhinged
Doors that held them captive
They sat out in the cold in Kasbah
And held vigil in Tahrir
Changing the tide
For dictators forever
They came from all generations
The ones who resisted French occupation
Held the door open to Bourguiba
And Ben Ali, urging capitulation.
They are the Saida Sadounis
Who have come out again this spring
They have inspired Asma Mahfoudh
In Egypt through Facebook gatherings
To march with their young compatriots
At the head of countless country women
And when their Yemeni counterpart
Was arrested in Sanaa, Tawakul Karman
Had an outraged country behind her
Forcing her captors to release her outright
As the call for freedom and democratic rights
Has swept across Syria while the world waits
As women leave homes leading populations
Out to defy snipers on rooftops.
In Bahrain, Saudi tanks might have crushed

Calls for freedom for now, but have not stifled
Voices of women in driving seats
In Riyadh, who steer their way
Through traditional roles, spurning perceived notions
As they chant, defiant and seize the day.

St Augustine's Church

with Regi Claire

Baklava and pastry with cream,
Semolina with pistachio, savouries
With parsley, tomato, nuts and chickpeas –
Laid out in a feast from Syria.

The father is distracted as his two-year-old
Runs into the church hall whenever
The door is opened by a new visitor.
His son has spotted a golden retriever
And is drawn to it like a magnet.
His father has to leave his stall
And follow. His son knows dog language
In that universal onomatopoeic translation,
Greeting the dog with 'Wow Wow.'
As he holds out a pleading hand, the golden eyes
Of this gentle giant turn on his tiny frame.
The little fan hugs himself and retreats
– Afraid but fascinated. The father kneels
And strokes the dog. His son steps forward
Cautiously and fingers one velvety ear.
The dog is still, inviting. The boy's fear
Evaporates. He squeals with delight
For now that he can stay by his father
Love and be loved, while the feast
Waits behind him, safe for now,
While his playmates left behind in Syria
Cower from snipers and swooping planes
In cities where children are targets of torture.

Medical Aid for Palestine

with Dr Swee

It was the third Saturday in November
The day when funds are raised for MAP.
Many years ago you had heard
Dr Swee speak, the intrepid
Orthopaedic surgeon, who worked
In the refugee camps from Beirut
To Jerusalem, treating the de-limbed,
Shelled, bombed, dislocated refugees
From Palestine. Today we heard her again
And her story of Haji, eighty-seven
And five times moved as her camp
Was flattened by a relentless surge
To occupy every home she tried to build
In the land of her fathers. Now her
Entire family of twenty-seven have been
Gunned down, but Dr Swee had
Saved one eleven-year-old grandson,
Amputeed but safe. But safe from what
Haji asks. Palestinians born now
For four generations and others to come
Are too tired of moving
And building and finding themselves
Alone by strange miracles
When their families erupt and explode
Around them, dismembered in unmarked
Graves and they are left shrouded
In a silence that the world

Cannot shatter as gunboats scour
The coast and tunnels are blocked
At gunpoint, the arteries
That might have taken food and medical aid
To those who remain, for now, in Palestine.

Women Vote in Jalalabad

Sameera and her mother-law
Had watched their naans fluff and turn brown
Inside their oven walls, before the
Last glow of the fire crackled and drowned.

They were there an hour before the polling began
In Jalalabad. Her mother-in-law in
Her blue burqa, her smiling eyes
Meeting Sameera's kohl-darkened expectancy.
Sameera's face caught the dull April sun while her body
Stood taut like a bowstring, its youthful vibrancy
Protected by the fall of her black nondescript robe.

They stood united under a plastic sheet they held
Against a desperate rain that muddied their flowing folds.
They joked and jostled and waited
With baited breath. The nervous April sun appeared
And faded as ballot papers disappeared.
Sameera and her mother-in-law's voices
Joined the adamant and vociferous queue
Of protesting mothers, daughters, widows and wives
Unwilling to let go of this moment in their lives
They had prayed for. They cheered
When the papers were delivered.

They walked out triumphant, the glistening tears
In her mother-in-law's eyes quivering
With a joy shared by Sameera, their ink-stained
Index fingers held aloft, defying the blood-stained
History of a nation whose women
Would not refrain from defending their domain.

Darkling I listen

It was in the stillness of midnight when the goslings
Had retired with mothers from their springtime dance
That my friend called me to step outside
While villages slept in the south of France.

Under the stars that lit a magnificent chapel
I could hear the deafening chorus of frogs, delirious
With song, who, my friend said, were tiny denizens
Of the world with voices ambitiously searching the stars.

But these were not the vocalists
She wished me to hear. She told me to walk round
To the other side of her home, and there I heard
A heavenly choir that drowned the sound

Of the throaty clamour that had surprised me earlier.
'Listen to the nightingales' my friend urged
And I did, hearing the trilling and twitter,
The chirping and whistling, the harmony that surged

Through the branches above me. I was bewildered.
I asked, 'but which one is the nightingale?'
I could hear the smile in her voice as she said
'Only nightingales sing at night.' And in the pale

Starlight, a line I had carried with me
All my life was suddenly suffused with illumination.
Of course, Keats could not have heard the bird
Singing in full-throated ease seeking its twilight destination.

He heard it in the stillness of the night
And I heard a full choir Ma, with a whole language
Of harmony, calling and answering
Improvising in ecstasy with freedom and courage

That comes with the knowledge of dominance
And excellence as all other songsters slumber.
So Ma, I heard the nightingales singing
Their full repertoire just as Keats had done one summer.

Anoushka in the Usher Hall

The Estonian conductor had been sedate
And contemplative as he let the haunting
Movements sweep over the converted.
After the interval, she came in, disarming
The gathering with a sweeping *namaste*
Reminiscent of her father's inclusive charm
Which you had witnessed in London and in Kolkata.

She took her place cross legged and elegant
On the floor of a special platform –
The vision of a modern Mirabai
Her instrument, her father's sitar
Which became her ethereal companion
As the conductor now danced to her Ragamala
The concerto of strings and brass
Tinkling with new rhythms that raced through their
Fingers and vibrated, displacing the air
The drummer's sticks cascaded like a Himalayan
Jhora, while the conductor was transported
To the land where the Ganga flows.

We heard the thunder before the lightening struck
We heard a gathering wind before the storm broke
We heard the first tingle of rain on still water
We heard the droplets sprinkle and cohere
We felt the clouds opening to send a benediction
To a land parched and waiting for the rain

It came pouring in a joyous composition
The Monsoons that moved a Scottish throng to cheer.

Your granddaughter in London

You will catch her on an early morning tube
Reading *Purple Hibiscus*, her *ghungrus*
In her jute bag, resting on her lap, still
For now. The world is shut out as she listens
To Idlewild on her ipod and enters another
Where patriarchy reigns as you knew it,
Being carried for her Saturday morning
Practice to Warren Street in a nameless hall
Where she will bring her birdflight agility
Of her ballet training to the grounded
Spins of a fusion of *gharanas*.

If you stroll through Covent Garden on a
Sunday afternoon, you will spot her
With her skinny latte, wickedly sweetened
With sugarfree hazelnut syrup, as she stops
To watch a street play or listens to a violinist
At the Piazza, before she and her friend
Debate what they will sample for their evening meal –
Lebanese, Vietnamese, Moroccan or Thai.

She has identified the character of the killer cell,
Danced her PhD in a carefully choreographed piece
Which you can watch on YouTube. It is a bid to save
Mother and baby before the stranglehold of
Eclamptic fits snuff out life, while her own
Stands on a fine balance of nutrition and strain.

Interlude

She was my mother

She was the Sheuli[1] in my wonderland
Discreetly tender, fragrantly appealing
She was my Swedish summer sun, hospitably warm –
My emblem of constancy and undying light,

She was my Zephyr, my refreshing energy
My liberating libretto, my compelling harmony
She was my Zodiac, my lucky songster
My winning universe, my orbiting dream

She was my Zenith, my sonic destination
My rainbow nation, my own Milky Way
She was my Rubicon, my intrepid defender
My splendid torchbearer, my true faith healer

She shone when all the stars left the stage
She stood, her head high, when the applause died.

1 A single petaled white flower with an orange stem, which blooms in autumn.

Letters to Other Mothers

Mothers All

They don't climb Everest from Nepal
They don't challenge every Munro
They don't swim across the Channel
They don't cycle round this orb

They are not the tree hammocking protesters
They are not the G summit marauders
They don't march silently in blood-stained Rangoon
They don't confront tanks in Tiananmen Square

They forego promotion and pay packets.
They stay at home. They are night watchers
Who feed and rock and calm to sleep
They tie their precious gifts to their back

Or stagger in tired pride, pushing our future
They are the bravest soldiers – marching on.

Brazenly – in Cafes

This is a new culture of concentrated inwardness
Where the marriage of a cup and thoughts
Flow onto paper or screen, undeterred
By fellow drinkers at other tables.

We have moved from smoky pubs
To smoke-free zones, from the mystery
Of dark interiors, droning voices and blaring
Football distraction, to seclusion.

From being the gin and tonic loner,
Or the kitchen table Brontë, propping notebook
Against recipe book, the reclusive Austen
Or the secretive Dickinson, carving, stitching

Words, away from the public gaze. We are brazen
Interlopers, claiming a space of our own in the metropole.

You cannot silence me

You can chalk a circle round my door
Command me sweep and mop my floor
But while you circumnavigate
You cannot contain me.

You can fold and wrap me from the gaze
Of curious sun and freedom's breeze
But while you wage your wars abroad
You cannot smother me.

Your secateurs can clip my wings
Your silver chain can cage me in
But while your warder's self stalks free
You cannot confine me.

The world will turn with my vision
You cannot silence me.

Abandoned: 1

He came home late with a smile
As broad as a river in spate
He had got the registrar's post in Brighton
– Was that why he was late? *Late*?
He looked surprised at my suggestion.
He had to leave early next morning
He told me briskly, rolling his sleeves up
To eat the steaming rice I spooned on his plate.
I would pack our bags after he'd eaten.
Ours? He was amazed. He was going alone.
I understood: he had to find a place for us,
Of course, he agreed, his thoughts whizzing past me.
He left with a swing in his hips, a dance in his step
I waited for his call in the silence and wept.

Restored: II

The rice no longer rattles at the bottom of the tin
The cold hollow of my fridge is a primeval cave
Echoing the folds of silence that have settled
Like dusty linen shrouds – wave on wave
Muffling my presence, shifting the dust
Allowing the rust to stifle my essence.
Then I hear the trill on my windowsill
Which needles effortlessly through my thin glass pane
Weaving through the shrouded rooms, with the thrill
Of a blackbird's passionate will, as it celebrates with
abandon
The onset of spring. It is my trumpet call
I smile at the mirror, my black tresses wave
In cascades as I brush them onto winsome defeat
There is a song on my lips as I trip down the stairs to
the street.

Urban Gothic: London during World War II

for Sara Wasson

The lights go out on Southwark Street
The blackout is now complete
Cars with muffled beams crawl past
Phantom shapes that grope and gasp.

In this stone forest of silhouettes
The wan moon swoons in pirouettes
Round rotting trees and wasted Heath
Its symphony, a dance of death.

There will be dancing on the streets
Once bombs create primordial piles
And girls from factories' smart retreats
Will click red shoes in rhythmic style

A ghost army marching in, to a soundless Doric tune
Will partner each dancing dream, unfolding beneath the
moon.

Eve: the Liberator

It was part of the divine strategy.
The Tree of Knowledge stood at
The epicentre of human validity,
Daring the adventurer and dreamer –
The Renaissance seeker of wisdom.
Eve knew that reason sets
The human race apart from
All creatures of creation.
But this power was dormant
While she and Adam roamed
Wide eyed with wonder
Innocent and unquestioning,
Experiencing a bliss as only the ignorant
Know. Yet her rational
Self sent deep currents
Coursing through her veins, lit
Sparks in her restless brain
Which directed a fiery longing
To her seeking tactile fingertips.
She had to reach out and pluck
The fruit that would take her
Beyond this Paradise, from
This eternal spring-like summer
Of her comfort zone, to challenge
The horizon. This was her
Destiny. She had to secure a future
For her progeny as the mother
Of mankind, for their intellectual

Engagement with the Creator
And his universe, of analytical
Debate with fellow citizens
Of a thinking, understanding
World of creative participation.

She did not want to mar
Adam with the blemish of
Rebellion. She would take the
Full first blame of crossing
The boundary that was set
As the obstacle to that inherent
Desire in man – the thirst for knowledge.
The benediction that she sought
In the rain of ideas, of truth
And explanation in this Eden
Where there were no indicators to tell her
How the trees grew, where the
Water came from, why the wind blew
And what lay beyond her bower.
She reached out for the apple
Of wisdom and once she had
Had a taste of the joy of knowledge
She did not want to be alone
With the secret, but in the
Generosity of her giving self
She shared her gift with her
Soul-mate and in that act of
Welcoming participation, she
Opened the doors of agency
And choice, of exploration
And discovery, of empirical

Endeavour to generations who
Could progress from ignorance,
Distinguish right from wrong
Learn to weave, build, plant and harvest
And establish that mantle
Of continuity with the Creator
In a meaningful exchange
That only the Creator could
Have foreseen and appreciated.

She

Kadambini,[1] immortalised by Tagore
Is Everywoman.
She is conceived without hankering
Grows without being wanted
And screams when she thrusts forward
To find her shrill note mingling
With the groans of a disapproving family
And a faltering mother's furtive care.

Her little hands learn to fetch and carry
Her father's newspaper and slippers
And balance his morning cup of tea
On a tipsy, crazy saucer, as her feet
Teach themselves not to go too fast
And spill or too slow to irritate.

She becomes a quick learner and a
Swift worker, swirling bedclothes to make
Beds that are tossed into shape and
Tucked into place with the
Hey presto magic of a Wallace and Gromit

1 Kadambini is the central character in a short story entitled 'The Living and the Dead' by Rabindranath Tagore. A young widow, Kadambini showers her affections on her brother-in-law's son. One day she is found dead and is carried by servants to the cremation ground on a stormy night, where she recovers. However, her bearers are frightened by her comeback and flee. They report that she has been cremated. But Kadambini's love for her nephew compels her to return to her in-laws' house where she is taken for a ghost and shunned. She is left with no option and commits suicide. The oft quoted line from Tagore is 'Kadambini had to die to prove she had not died' and has become emblematic of many a woman's unwonted existence.

Precision-filled, mechanical world.
Only in hers she is the machine –
Efficient, obedient, immaculate.

Her brothers know that they can
Bring home football soiled
Strips, mud-splattered trainers
And line the house floor
With socks and their rucksacks
For her to gather and rub clean
Tumble-wash, unpack and reassemble
Today, for their next game tomorrow.

        She can make her wants simple
        Her appetite small
        Bypass the nourishment
        And wait in the stalls
Mixing abilities in tired
Schoolrooms; saying cheers
To her brothers who gleam
Amongst blazered peers.
        She has a few choices –
        Of love and a cradle
        Of demanding attention
        And a lifetime of Babel –
Or marriage and drawn dreams,
Of shopping and mopping
Of lost sleep and long hours
Youth giving at its seams –
        ...Or if she can scrape through
        To grab one last space
        In the ruthless rat-race

Of uni and grade grind
She might just make do
To become the smart
Role model for young ones
With swelling breasts
Bursting with ambitions –
She'll have gusto in her speech rhythms
A swing to her hipline
Shadows under eye makeup
Holding back the brine.
She'll be the wizard cook
The bewitching wife
The mum of the dark ages
Who has forgotten a good life.
She will become the
Middle-aged embarrassment
Of her teenage entourage
And a perfect ensemble
Of a modern collage...
Still running errands for her father
Surreptitiously tidying
Her mother's grey hair;
Standing proxy for her
Brother as a niece weds in time
For the baby nearly there.
And if she is lucky
Her pressure may rise
To make her heart burst
And then all around her
Will recognise her at last
As the woman who sustained

Them, and feel bereaved
Of one who remained
Alive for the living –
Unwanted, unnoticed
Unidentified till dead –
Like Tagore's Kadambini.

My Aunt Marge

My Aunt Marge lives on the edge
Of the village in her little white cottage.

She had waved goodbye, handing a bouquet
To her brother Hector over sixty years ago
With tears in her eyes and a brave
Smile on her lips, when he went to the War.

He never came back, though a telegram did
Saying what a great hero he was. So he stood
Smiling on her dresser in his smart uniform
And as a little boy on a bicycle in a glass cabinet
In her chintz curtained living room
And she spoke to him every morning as she did
To Roger, with whom she sat hand in hand
On a studio couch: she in a floral dress
And he in his dark uniform with wings on his
Shoulders, both smiling hopefully for a future
With no War, when they would have married
If only his plane had not crashed
In that village near the city, far away –
The name of which slipped her memory
As did many things these days...

So she told these two young men of what
She would be up to and what she
Would buy, and what she would
List as messages for her milkman
Who was a good lad, bringing things
To her door. She didn't go to these
Big places with rows and rows of things
That set her head whirling.
The little things that she needed
Were at the corner shop –
Her tea leaves in a box, her Robinson's
Barley and marmite, digestive biscuits
And corned beef and condensed milk in cans.

And at night without blackouts
And sirens, she sat watching the
Patterns of intricate flowers on her carpet,
Dreaming of the exotic lands where
Her Hector and her Roger had gone
And now lay, mixed in the dust
While she remained where they left her
On the edge of the village in the
Little white cottage, while the rest of the
Street changed and others moved on.

My Monimashi

Monimashi, a name that resonates with love
Monimashi, who was born to give and serve
Monimashi, who embraced my parents' world
Monimashi, who was there in every fold
Of our lives, a presence larger than life,
My aunt, a mother, a sister, a wife.

What will the world be like without Monimashi?
When my parents married, she was the pigtailed
Schoolgirl in a frock, who became their daughter.
She was undaunted and free like a spry pony
The only girl who could score at ease with the boys,
Playing football or racing a wheel along a road.
She could challenge any treetop and row a boat,
Steer her father's Chevrolet and swim across a moat –
My Monimashi, with the sweetest smile that won
Every heart that experienced her sun.

And how do I start to describe what she meant to us?
A gentle, caring essence of our very existence
Loyal to the core, a person we could trust –
Reliable, unassuming, generous without pretence.

She was the pole star of our skies
Through our post-Partition struggle to survive
She was the embankment against tides
Of menacing change, ready to revive
Lost hopes and fading dreams in all around her
Knitting together family and friends who surround her
To celebrate a life, a flame, a touch of pure

Olympian glory, that will burn
Whenever goodness is born
In women like Monimashi, who live to make a difference
In other people's lives, ushering in their dawn.

And how will I remember my Monimashi?
I will remember the champion shot-put thrower
The javelin wielder, the sprinting sportswoman
Jubilant as Number One prize winner
In her red bordered sari, her *anchal*
Tucked neatly into her youthful waist.
She was my smart NCC[1] Major, with her
Winning stripes and her clicking heels
A tremendous shot, who could never
Aim a gun at a living object.
She was the intrepid Warden
Of the Girls' Hostel, and her glance
Froze every would-be Romeo of Jalpaiguri.
Yet men followed her lissom figure
Longingly, knowing she was unattainable,
Her dignified reserve hiding her essentially
Shy nature. *This* was my Monimashi –
My academic, my roving geographer,
Studying altimeters, peering through theodolites,
Tracing maps and filming hanging valleys;
My trekker, my mountaineer, my scarved,
Sunglassed Monimashi on Darjeeling heights.

How will we go on train journeys again
Without your thoughtful care
That calmed uncertain nights
Across unknown terrain?

1 The National Cadet Corps of India.

When you took up work in the next town
It hurt to let you go
And weekends became a solace
When we saw you once more.

Your cooking was proverbial
Your generosity untold
Your forgetfulness was real
Lighting smiles all round.

And then you built upwards
From the foundations of your heart
To accommodate Ma, Baba
As you couldn't live apart.
And even in Kolkata
You were never far away
When Baba needed eye-drops
Or Ma's femur broke one day.

Why did you have to suffer
When through your giving days
You relieved pain in others
In every possible way?

Once when I was lost in Park Circus Maidan
You ran around demented till you found me again.
I can still feel your heart throb as you held me tight,
I was drenched as you sobbed with tears of delight.

You gave me my first watch, my first camera
You were my new year, my saviour, my second mother.

How can I mark time now and see it pass
Or glue together snapshots of you amidst us?

Whenever we drive through the forests of North Bengal
Whenever we light a lamp in a Himalayan bungalow
Whenever we dig up the wilderness and tame it to flower
Whenever we dip our feet in the turbulent water
Of a virgin spring and hear a song echo round the hills
Whenever there are events to organise – of excursions
And picnics, international seminars and weddings,
Whenever there are celebrations and funerals, lives to repair
And bring together, we will remember
Monimashi who was always there
For others. She was my mother's rock,
My father's sapphire, precious and rare
She was her daughter's bunyan tree
Her husband's watchful sentinel
Her family's guardian angel
Her friends' safety net –
Our very anchor and dock.

I wanted you Monimashi to come to me
So that I could spoil you as you had spoilt me –
This time, in my Scottish city.

Everywhere I turn
My eyes burn with longing.
And Monimashi you are always there
Walking towards me, standing by me,
Watching over me. I feel your quiet pace
I see your beautiful face lighting up my world,
My harried days and wakeful nights, with your grace.

Shamsad Rahim

For the Bangladeshi community
You were their mother hen,
Protective and compassionate
Holding them under your generous wing.

For your friends who knew you
You were their full moon
Your broad smile their welcome
That made their hearts sing.

For your own loving family
You were their pole star
Reliable and constant
Who watched everything.

For your colleagues who valued you
You were their corner stone
Your presence an essence
Like a fresh mountain spring.

For your two cherished countries
Of Scotland and Bangladesh
You were a torchbearer
Of eternal wellbeing.

A Breaker

for Payal and her mother Jharna

Love and the sea seem far away
Playing somewhere beyond my territory
I stand alone, the wavelets trinkle
Like ankle bells; between my toes –
Gentle amorous bites demanding to
Embrace and reach higher, but I do not give in.
I see the tall shadow before it sees me –
Darkly handsome, dashing and unafraid
Ready to try its tricks, to sweep over me
Scoop down and pick me up in a passion
Of surging swirl, lifting me off my feet
My balance tripped in moments
Move beyond control and count, and I
Melt in the smothering arms of this new
Sensation. The world is subsumed
In a silence of commitment. Windows of reality
Lost in this dreamlike ease. The strength
Of this new conquest slackens and loosens
Its grip as quickly as it had clutched me.
In seconds it leaves me bare, my nakedness
A glare as the sun burns on my salt body
Love and the sea have retreated to play
Far away and I have reclaimed my territory
Letting the sting of the mighty breaker
Wash over me like an inevitable big wave
That must come and retreat as is its
Nature, while I will stand and observe,
With no regrets or any desire to retreat.

The Song of a Gypsy

I am your gypsy
Brown as a berry
A berry you can't eat –
Not because it's tart
But because it's not red and sweet
Like your cherry.

I'm as brown as the bark
Of the beech in your driveway
Which you might want to hack
Down and clear away.

I can steal upon you in the night
And camp along your river's brink
And surprise you in the morning light
When you open your curtains and shrink.

I can read your pretty palm
And foretell your fortune
I can give you a soothing balm
And a hypnotising tune.

I can transport your bairns
To never never lands
In stories they've never heard,
Of deeds they've never dared.

But I will not cross your fence
Of a prison gate
My crystal ball is in my tent
Where I will sit and wait

Till you can drop your deep-set fears
And come to me at will
And I will wipe my past of tears
And gladly share my skills.

Living Joy

confessions to a mother

Her name was Joy which describes her so well
She was fun to be with, always ready for a laugh.
We did weird things together when I was at my Gran's
We never met at our front door
I'd always look out for her from Gran's kitchen window
Where I'd be sipping lemonade, waiting
For her dark bunches, bobbying up and down
As she swung over the turnstile at the end
Of our meadow. And as she skipped over the green,
I ran out and climbed over the fence
And we both raced to the river, to look
For stones that we could throw into it to see the
Crystal water turn foamy as it splashed into
A hundred ripples. We would go looking
For eggs that mother birds had left unguarded
And Joy could climb the most unclimbable trees
Reaching the top till she said
She could breathe the clear blue sky air
And I'd have to plead with her not to stay there
Too long for the branch to crunch under her weight
And crack. It never did, though she swayed
And bent it till I froze and then she'd always come
Down laughing, telling me that I had her
Baby sister's girlish heart, though I was a boy.

Joy showed me the dent in the bush on the edge of
Our shrubbery, through which a frequent visitor
Of a fox came looking for Gran's hens. She could
Be as quiet as a mouse, as we waited for
The night time badgers that ambled across
Our back garden on calm April mornings.

She was a wizard at building campfires
Where Gran would let us roast sausages
On forks she let us have, which we ate
Burnt and charred, with thick mugs
Of muddy tea that Joy coaxed out of a tin kettle
That she boiled over the flaming woodpile.

She was part of my farm life
A lass that was at ease
With the wild horses and butterflies.
I was waiting for her to grow into
A joyous woman, whom I could
Ask to marry, to bring her joy
Into my life in this busy city.
But I guess she was meant to
Remain where she was, never
To be torn from the glen she was born
In, for one summer she felt a pang
As she rode her brown mare –
And as her left hand touched her heart,
She turned her mischievous
Wondering eyes on me as I stood
Watching her flying bunches. Her
Right hand still held the reins

As the horse came charging past
Me and she lurched over, a smile
Of surprise beginning round the corners
Of her mouth. I instinctively stepped
Forward to feel the pressure of her
Body, warm and exciting, invade mine
As we toppled over on the grass
And the horse galloped on.
I realised that Joy's heart
Had stopped just as her folks knew
It would one day,
Experiencing the joy of living
For she knew that she had not
Long to live – her one secret
That she had not shared with me.

Laure

You were away once in sunny southern France
Where you fled sometimes when the North Sea
Wind chased your blithe spirit to retreat and recover.
You were sorry that you would miss the welcome
You had planned for my parents on their arrival
Here, as their plane had made a U-turn as a cyclone
Gripped the Bay of Bengal. When they arrived two days
Later once the storm had relented, they were greeted
By a surprise gift in a pendulum of a plastic bag that
had been left
Swinging on our door handle. It was a lemon drizzle
cake mixed with your
Mediterranean candour, sweetened by your rare
affectionate nature,
Flavoured by your sophisticated splendour and offered
with your consummate
Skill of forging friendships across nations, sparkling
with your joie de vivre
Which made my reticent mother declare it was the best
she had ever tasted.

Who Was the Boy?[1]

I saw the outstretched hand
Before I saw the face, a wrinkled claw
That echoed the sorrow-streaked cheeks.
I met her eyes, which widened with wonder
'Betia' she said, with anguish and pleading
'My Betia!' Her hand was now urgently
Seeking more than my small change.
I shrank back. Her hand withdrew
With alarm to stifle her shriek.
The bus came, my friend and I
Scrambled in, the coins cool in my fist.
'Do you know her?' she asked
'No' I shrugged, as I glimpsed her ragged
Body, tiredly pulling a little boy away.
'But who was the boy?' I wondered
As my mind jerked back to that night
I had consciously submerged for a decade.

The engines were revving when we were
Hauled in the darkness on waiting trucks
Urged by the distant thunder
Of an approaching mob. My mother's *dupatta*
Had fallen from her head. 'Stop' she cried,
'I have to go back. I forgot my Betia's jewellery.'
'Ammu, don't go' I sobbed.
'Won't be a moment, Beta,' her soft hand
Brushed my cheek and hair in a swift caress.

1 Inspired by Jyotirmoyee Devi's story, 'Chheleta' (The Boy).

'Wait, my Bibi has gone inside,' my father's
Voice begged above the din of an audible roar.
'We can't wait, they are too near' was the verdict
Of the social worker. 'She'll be in another truck'
A neighbour soothed as we fled into the night.

For the first few years after crossing the border
My father scoured camps and hospitals,
Looking for my mother. In my day dreams
I was focused on studying to become a teacher –
An empowered women in my new country.
But in my nightmares, I felt her last caress
And saw the flames swallowing my mother's memory
As our truck journeyed through a splintered nation.

I went back, again and again, to the bus-stop
Asked in the shops around, had they seen her?
'The beggar woman who haunted these streets?
'No.' She had disappeared like the tears of many
Ravaged women. But who was the boy with her?
I never did have a brother, did I?

Will you remember me?

My fists and kicks brought a smile to your lips
When the weight of waiting made you heavy and slow
My angry scream and protesting entry
Brought tears that shone with your glad heart's glow

My every new word from the simple 'moon'
To the polysyllabic 'butterfly'
Was a new star on your widening horizon –
My potential as boundless as the noontide sky

My ascent from a crawler
Steady for precious moments
As I balanced on my little feet
Was your supreme fulfilment

My every uncertain step,
Awkward and tilting
Was the mark of a champion athlete
Promising and uplifting.

So when my fists started to speak for me
And my kicks became my victory
When my stagger was the swagger
Of sodden drunken vigour

When my uncertain steps wavered
From drug dens and favours
Brought to you as trophies
Of my new life of ease

Your tears were no jewels
Your face lost its true smiles
For your horizon saw disaster
As your stars lost their lustre.

So I left you one dark night
When the gang's whistle called
Your door was unhinged
And your whole life was stalled.

So if you know I am out there
Prowling in the dark
Will you have a light on
To entice my steps back?

If you hear I have shot a gun
With cold aim and killed
Will you bake me a fruit cake
And see my bath is filled?

When you hear I lurk in woods
And plunder the next village
Will you keep my slippers warm
To honour your own pledge?

When I light a blaze that
Explodes and turns a market to rout
Will you light a candle
At your window and continue to gaze out

Looking for my stagger
Listening for my words
Will you lay your table
With a plate for your flown bird?

And if you hear I was in a crowd
That crushed women and devoured
Their many-petaled splendour
In the fumes of civil war

And if you know that children have been
Slain and maimed by me
While vultures watch in rotting fields
Where flames I light, reign free

Would you pick me out in a crowd
And know me as your own
Or would you turn and walk away
Steadily from your son?

Awakening

Every night I play the same game –
Count odd objects in the room
The stairs I climb to bed
The movement of my toothbrush,
Muttering, he will come home /
He won't come home tonight –
Playing tick-tack, a teenager
Plucking petals from a daisy,
Blotting out one persistent image
Of him lying with others
In a ring of oblivion, somewhere
In the city, his eyes
Lustreless, his face cadaverous,
His youthful flush drained
Viciously like a gushing river
Surprised by a big dam
That twists its sinews to bend
To foreign will and leave an old course –
A bed forced nakedly dry and prospectless.

The contrast is my younger one,
Hyperactive like a squirrel, scurrying
Around with an expectant glint, looking
For gains to glean, eager, romping,
Unafraid and briskly businesslike.
I fall asleep on the margins of darkness
Acceding to light, when I hear a young
Voice calling out his name. Their names
Are similar, given as pet-names

In playful affection before they had grown
Characteristics to fit our claims.
My expectation flutters like a tethered parrot
Pulsating to be unchained to breath free.
Has my older one stumbled home?
No, it is a summons to rouse my
Younger one to join the swimmers
Before the heat haze raises the populace.
Why can't you wake up, I say
Without your friends disturbing me everyday?
I don't want to go, he answers, his voice lazy,
Lost in a dreaming daze. Do you want
The neighbourhood awake? I demand
And he staggers out, pulling on his shirt
I know, his round face puffy with missed sleep.

An hour later, his friend comes back,
His eyes dilated, his voice rasping
– My prize swimmer, sank like a tanker
As cramps constrained his surprised body, he sobs.
As I crumple to my knees, I see the awakening
Horror on my older son's face
Who has crawled back from a cocaine cruise,
His unseeing eyes opened to the unrealisable
Opportunities, snuffed out indelicately
At the bottom of an unfeeling lake
Of his whizzing rocket of a younger brother.

Light where the sun sets

I don't know when I had stopped
Hearing my own voice.
My co-patriots' slogans
Frozen like thousands
Of Munch screams,
Creating vibrations
Of colour contours
That curled round
Police battle shields,
Batons and barrels
As the noon sun
Slinted my vision
And I was dragged
By my plait to a waiting van,
Rained upon by sharp
Boots and stony knuckles.

It all happened like a
Silent film around me –
Was I at the epicentre
Or was I a spectator
Invisible to them?
My body a sacrificial
Animal that needed
To be cleansed,
Claimed and offered
Multiple times till
I lost count, my senses
Dimmed, my voice
Drowned in a monastic cell.

One day which seemed
No different from the
Lighted shaft above
My steel cage, I was
Marched to a hearing
Where a crowd waited
To see me walk away
With startling cameras
Marking my retreat to a
Waiting boat from which
I saw the mist swaddling
My continent as I headed
For freedom's song.

I know I will sing again
In this lonely warehouse
Behind barbed wires
From where I watch
Children bounce across
The village green
Free from my agonised
Glance, my silent voice –
For now. But tomorrow
My advocate will bring
Me my own weapons
And I will know the sweetness
Of words on crisp paper
In this new prison
Softened by the twilight.

Light a candle for me

written on request for a seminar at the University of Edinburgh

You used my name
To set this country aflame
When my image became
Interchangeable with the deity –
The object of your piety,
Yours to defend, your Devi,
Your mother, your dignity.

My feminine will flows
Here in the Ganga and Jamuna
In the Tapti, the Godavari
The Narmada and the Kaveri
Indulging one male counterpart
To play his turbulent part
As Bramha's wayward son.

Your poets and politicians
Your artists and journalists
Have found inspiration
In my creative role,
My maternal essence
That permeates this nation
As the *shakti* that sustains it.

But your ambivalence has
Amazed me. It was on
My body that you marked
Your territorial right,
Abducted my daughters
Violated me in my own house
And encouraged my honourable

Death in wells where
I was stifled by the bodies
Of my sisters, not by the water
That I had drawn to quench
Your parched souls when
I was allowed to be your
Mother in an undivided nation.

Now six decades later
When liberalisation has
Opened doors for India's
Billion to dream of a share
In this boom, my daughters
Come to the capital of a proud
Nation, burgeoning and free

But are we free
To walk, without your
Leering glance, your grasping
Claws, your prowling presence,
Your tribal fervour that revels
In the gang violence of wolf packs
With an appetite for spoils?

Your politics is played
In our villages through
Intimidation and rape, the coward's
Weapon, the feudal landlord's
Tradition carried over
In a nation we had hoped
To build as a modern bastion.

From the terror of Mussulmen
In rural India, from
The brutalised police
Of *moffussil* towns,
We have sought refuge
And dignity in our big cities –
But today we encounter the violation

That ravages our grand capital
Where 7.00pm is the curfew hour
For women to return and cower
At home; where public transport
Is the public spot for concerted
Crime, in the knowledge that law
Remains the rapists' staunch protector.

As convictions will not take place
In a country where false witnesses
Can be easily construed, while truth
Is stifled by terror perpetrated
By the very institutions that should
Have protected us in this new India
Where we should have walked free

I am your daughter

You invested thousands
To make that one journey
To clear the path
For your dreamt-of son.
This was your smart plan –
To avoid paying more
For me, in case I was born.
Your excuse was my dowry
Which you had constructed
In a highrise that rises
In its ugly overpowering
Unsanctified illegal existence
On a non-existent foundation
That cannot sustain love or dignity.

Yes, you were under pressure
From husband and in-laws
From a whole community
Born of their mothers
To block my right
Of entry into this sunlit world.

You stole my breath
You stifled my shriek
You snuffed me out
After I had sprouted.

You thought you were
Done with me. You came
Back empty, a ready vessel
For the son you will never hold
In your intimate cradle
Or longing arms. I return to haunt
Your idle noonday dreams
I hover over your humid
Nights. I toss your stormy
Thoughts. I taunt your
In-laws. I am the presence
That withers standing crops
Without warning. I am the
Accomplice of the burning sun
That leaves the rivers panting
For water, begging to flow.
I am the lightning that
Strikes the laden mango tree.
I am the *shakti* in the cloud
That heaves the sea to rise
And swallows you and yours.

My absence creates your
Hungry repressed marauders
To wander in packs
Seeking victims in
The forests of Madhya Pradesh
The hotels of Agra
The mill compounds of Mumbai
The public buses of Delhi
The villages of Uttar Pradesh –

Because you stopped
My journey to your
World, *my* world, where
I could put the balance
Right and provide
Your friend's son
With the partner
He could have had
If you had not scraped
My heart out to create
The gap that has set
The wolves to wander free.

I return mother, your
Daughter, again and again
To remind you that I will
Not be killed in vain
But will set this country
Aflame in a conflagration
She has started and
Cannot contain.

Rupsha

When I was a little girl
I loved the music soirees in our living room
My parents' duet – a near-forgotten war song
Remembering with nostalgia a lost Bengal
– *My mother sitting by the fence of rushes*
Crying at the impending reality of her son leaving
For the War – the haunting melody moved my
Young girl's vision – *It's a long way* – not to
Tipperary, but – *to the banks of the Rupsha*
River where I had my playroom...
And down the meandering path I took my leave.
Though my heart resists today, my memory
Sneaks back and lingers there –
It is to this memory that I owe Rupsha.

Rupsha, whose root word *'Rup'* conjures
Beauty – *Ruposhi* – the beautiful
– An offering of love and devotion, like a garland
Of jasmine draped round *Ruposhi Bangla*
– My parents' beautiful Bengal
Which for them was east Bengal
The soil of which Rupsha replenishes.

The Rupsha which adorns like a
Blossom, Ruposhi Bangla's poet's
Verse, Jibananada's[1] oft-quoted line –
Merging her with Meghna in Rupsha's
Dark waters, which today hide
Passion in my Rupsha's eyes.

So can I turn round and say
What's in a name?
When naming my daughter
Has captured a haunting melody,
Retrieved the memory of a lost land
And subsumed the magic of poetry.

1 Jibananda Das is a poet of both Bengals and his famous collection, *Ruposhi Bangla* (written in 1934, published posthumously in 1957), features the river Rupsha.

For Nisha and Ben on your wedding day

It could have been an icy first meeting
But his warm steadying hand
At her elbow, kept her on her skating feet
All evening. He was a stranger from another land

Handsome and debonair
Without the flair of the practiced charmer
She was the doe-eyed beauty,
Cautious and observant and no flighty dreamer.

The soothing richness of hot chocolate
Sealed the evening with comforting thoughts.
Phone numbers were exchanged
And meetings arranged
Which followed with the calm precision
Of definitive seasons and firm decisions.

The test came when she was in hospital
And he hovered, an anxious, constant presence
On her semi-conscious horizon
An ever-present flame which became the essence
Of her bolstered faith in humanity.

Trials came and evaporated –
An eight-hour wait in Paris en-route
To Mount Pleasant was exacerbated
One cold Christmas with the son's fiancée
Arriving amidst the Michigan gentry

Without her suitcase of sartorial elegance
Reduced to borrowed feathers on her first entry
To this close-knit family whose warmth
Ensconced her amidst the Mid-West's snow.
When her suitcase did arrive, they demanded
She change every hour to catch the catwalk glow.

From one vast country, you have
Travelled to another sub-continent
Your third and last, where you had the pleasure
Of eating *golgappas* to your heart's content –

Aunts and Uncles along the Atlantic
And the Indian Ocean have shown the devotion
To two who are obviously destined
For each other for a life of fruition.

You were blessed by a random zealous priest
Months ago in bustling sunny Mumbai
And the mantras have worked magic
As the pilot takes the wheel in a well-planned
Flight to IT, to wed his zoologist
Academic manager with more than a pretty face.

Her mother will tell you, her gentleness distinguishes
Her from her tiny tot years. Her father has found
Her undemanding, self-effacing sweetness, endearing.

We have seen his stalwart dedication
His disarming smile, his steady flame
Matching his steadying hand
That promises to stay the same.

We know you will not sit still
But continue your keep fit regime
Of running and skating
And your cultural rounds that light meaningful dreams.

But today signifies the moment of giving
When months of active sharing
And conscientious loving find fulfilment
In a sacred exchange of vows committed to conjoined
  living.

Nisha, you deserve the sweetness
Your own life has engendered

Ben, you deserve the radiance
Of care your own self has expended.

We wish both Everest glory, and the
Extended light of temperate summer days
We wish you golden harvests of Michigan plenty
And the merging of three continents in your romantic
  gaze.

To Tithi on your wedding day

When you sat on the Mughal style stage
Which had startled Sheraton's modern
5 Star standard with its Durbari splendour,
You brought the aesthetics of your eastern

Inheritance to complement the grandeur
You eclectically chose from your western
Upbringing, to create a seamless fusion
Marked by the distinctive flavour of your person.

Your Uncle Neil said you were like Cleopatra –
A captivating queen whose glamour
Held your aunties and uncles glowing
With pride at what you capture

In your presence. But for me you are
Not only Farha as the world knows you,
But the Tithi of your mother's tender
Thoughts, a name which signifies the due

Moment when you arrived, auspicious and true,
Almost two decades ago. I remember the day
When you danced around the sofa where your mother
And I sat reminiscing about Kolkata, mangoes and
mishti doi,[1]

The Monsoons and the songs that flowed from
The land of the Ganga to this city of seven hills
Which is yours to enrich and transform
With your designer's eye, your aesthetic will

1 A delectable sweet yoghurt typical to Bengal.

That you have brought to every fold of the Reza
Household, and you will now carry as a gift
To the Khalid home to imbue and enhance
Their generous vivacity which is uplifting

For us all to know that you will continue to glow
In their presence, your essence augmenting
Their enlightened world. You are the centripetal
Force in your family, taking on the daunting

Task of playing multiple roles – your father's girl,
A caring sibling, a fun companion to Ramiz,
A second mother to Ashif and your mother's
Constant comfort. You are the zephyr, the breeze

That brings good news, the promise of freshness –
The uplifting joie de vivre that has transfused
Your dancing feet, your creative choreography,
And led you to choose a career women don't often choose

Following in your father's footsteps, but taking a further
Step forward to being an architectural engineer.
You have been a central light on stage, and I was proud
When the audience assumed I was the mother

Of two beautiful daughters in you and Rupsha.
But though I cannot quite claim to be a mother
To a Cleopatra, I can bask in the glow of the rainbow
That you are, bridging two worlds, the harbinger

Of warm skies. Usman has chosen well and we commend
His good taste. And we can see that Tithi, you have found
Your soul-mate and a loving family and we know you will
Be valued in your new role and loved and bound
As only love can bind.

Mariam

The stadium is full. The roar of voices is from a
fascinated crowd.
But this is no match between players confronting
Each other in a game of active participation
Played by rules that both sides know and understand.
This is a grim sport, where one is the condemned victim –
Unheard, undefended against a mighty state that
Is all powerful, like a god, but not all merciful and
compassionate.

This crowd has gathered to witness justice being done
To a woman who has dared to kill a man who was intent
On snuffing her life out in a frenzy of ownership and
utter control.
She does not hear the tumult now. A silence surrounds her
As if she is floating in an underwater film where she cannot
Hear the world above the waves or feel the sun on her skin
As she has never known the warmth of its nurturing rays.

She stumbles on the flowing folds of her burqa, her hands
Tied under it behind her back, making her gait awkward
As the man behind her shoves her forward with the hard
Nozzle of his poised gun which she feels against her aching
Back. She kneels as ordered and holds her head steady,
Her mind on the little girl and her mother who are now free
From his imaginative torture, free to leave and free to grow.

She remembers the Friday revelry in another country
Where men walk to the city square to marvel and revel
In beheadings and crucifixion. She remembers reading
Of a sister being stoned somewhere by a decree
Passed by one man in a remote village where he plays god.
She knows that across the Atlantic, perhaps at this very
moment,
One man sits in a chair drugged with a lethal injection

And another is hung by an executioner in a closed prison
In the name of civilisation and justice on the other side
of the globe.
Is it condonable when a modern nation with a collared
judge decrees
It and it occurs in a private sanctioned place, supported
by the
State machine? Is this more barbaric because of the
spectacle –
A public circus inviting a multitude's gaze? She does not
hear the swish of the
Sword. She does not wail, spoiling for once the sport of
these joy starved men.

Bhopal now

My baby sleeps
Dreaming of Wonderland.
My boy and girl weep
Cramped by burning pain

My mother-in-law keeps vigil,
Waving a weary fan
To soothe their dewy dampness,
Pushing back a wispy strand
From her bleary eyes,
Flinching from their fiery itch.

Her husband's ashes have
Been mixed with my
Husband's, in water that
Races like death's own chariot,
Galloping through the city
Having surfaced from earth's
Bowels where it has churned
Through our well waters

And now invites the clouds
To join in this invidious war
Against a defenceless city

A reminder of that cloud which
Seeped into our unwary waking dreams
One December night

Contaminating my baby's
Dreams of Wonderland
Forever.

I am that child

I am the child
Who couldn't see
My mother's dreams
Fulfilled in me
Which were consumed
In the white heat
Of annihilation
And defeat.
I died before
I was born
Not once, but twice
Before my dawn
In Hiroshima
And four days later
In Nagasaki's
Vicious crater.

I have breathed
In Warsaw's streets
A budding artist
In grim retreats
A dreaming Amal[1]
Who would await
A King's letter
Before his fate
Took him on that
One last train
To a destination
That would remain
My life's final stop
Where my shout
Would in a furnace
Be snuffed out.

1 Amal is the young boy in Rabindranath Tagore's play, *The Post Office*, who is very ill but touches everyone with his goodness and positive attitude to life. He awaits the King's letter with the optimistic credulity of a child. Tagore's *The Post Office* was directed by Dr Janusz Korczak and acted by the children at the orphanage in the Jewish ghetto in Warsaw to let the children know dignity in the face of death, in spite of a Nazi ban on the performance. A packed audience was moved by a powerful performance of the play in 1942. The children were later taken by train to Treblinka with Dr Korczak accompanying them, where they all were exterminated.

And I would rise
Once again
As the child
Born of pain
My mother's body
A territory
Marked for a mob's
Victory.
When communal violence
Sent shock waves
And millions walked
To mass graves

My begging hands
In foreign land
My mother's rags
A nation's flag
Her sagging breasts
Her streaked face
Her shame inflicted
By her race
When one cleaved nation
Splintered, sprang
To pick its fragments
I began
My journey
Through hungry nights
On freedom's pavements
In lonely flight
My mother and I
Fugitives
From life, which
Does not forgive.

I am the child
Scorched by flames
That woke the world
To voice its shame
When powerful nations
Clashed on soil
That was not theirs
To despoil
My paddy fields
Were ransacked
My peasants rose
To fight back
Amidst that bid
For dignity
A nurturer
Gave birth to me
I am the child
Of Saigon
Born of love
As wars waged on

You will find me
In Bangkok's sprawl
Behind the brothel's
Secret walls,
In Korea's
Closed retreats
An abandoned child
Playing on the streets
Each time my mother
Was embraced
By a GI's

Loving grace
My mixed heritage
Was a disgrace
When my blue eyes
Lit my brown face

I am the child
With sharpened bones
Made angular
In hunger's zone
I see the shadow
Of my death
In a vulture's
Bated breath.

I am that child
Who daily walks
Desert miles
To feed her stock.

I am the child
Who knows air-raids
Plays with danger
And grenades.
A defunct tank
Is my playpark
With gunfights we
Make our mark.

I am the child
Who wakes at dawn
To light the fire
Cook the corn.
I seed the fields
I feed the babe
I scour for water
For my tribe.
My generation
Stands bereft
Of parents
Who have all left
As AIDS invades
And in one stroke
Severs Africa
From hope.

So we are now
Easy recruits
Swaggering
Through jungle routes
Weighed by guns
Forced to confront
The firing line
On battle fronts.

I am the child
You will see
Shining your boots
In your city.

I am the child
Who dives and swims
Like free fish
On ocean's whims.

I wash your car
I sweep your trains
I pour your tea
I clean your drains.

You step over my
Sleeping bones
On platforms, pavements –
Freedom's homes.

I long to ride
The wind and run
To swim the ocean
Feel the sun.
I am the child
You taught shame
Your muffling veil
Hid my small frame.
I long to steal
Into your schools
But know the terror
Of your rules.
I still can hear
My mother's screams
Stoned to death
In my worse dreams.

I am the child –
My cries unheard
Invisible
To border guards.
I pass freely,
Changing hands
Across the lines
Of many lands.
My parents' faces
Soon grow dim
Sold many times
Till I reach him
Who has a whip
And rotten bread
Who drives me on
From a harsh bed.

I am the child
Who crouches, cowed,
On racing camels
To a cheering crowd
Petrified as
My beast runs
With my puny body
Dried by the sun.

I am the child
Who wears high heels
Smudged lipstick
And makes street deals.

I find glue
I find the haze
I find the fumes
That glaze my gaze.

Today I sit
On London's streets
I note the many
Thousand feet
This is my own
Silent retreat
My face is hidden
From your gaze
My placard
Blocking my image
And if by chance
You cast your glance
You will note my address
Is 'Hungry and Homeless'.

Luath Press Limited

committed to publishing well written books worth reading

LUATH PRESS takes its name from Robert Burns, whose little collie Luath (*Gael.*, swift or nimble) tripped up Jean Armour at a wedding and gave him the chance to speak to the woman who was to be his wife and the abiding love of his life. Burns called one of 'The Twa Dogs' Luath after Cuchullin's hunting dog in Ossian's *Fingal*. Luath Press was established in 1981 in the heart of Burns country, and now resides a few steps up the road from Burns' first lodgings on Edinburgh's Royal Mile.

Luath offers you distinctive writing with a hint of unexpected pleasures.

Most bookshops in the UK, the US, Canada, Australia, New Zealand and parts of Europe either carry our books in stock or can order them for you. To order direct from us, please send a £sterling cheque, postal order, international money order or your credit card details (number, address of cardholder and expiry date) to us at the address below. Please add post and packing as follows: UK – £1.00 per delivery address; overseas surface mail – £2.50 per delivery address; overseas airmail – £3.50 for the first book to each delivery address, plus £1.00 for each additional book by airmail to the same address. If your order is a gift, we will happily enclose your card or message at no extra charge.

ILLUSTRATION: IAN KELLAS

Luath Press Limited
543/2 Castlehill
The Royal Mile
Edinburgh EH1 2ND
Scotland

Telephone: 0131 225 4326 (24 hours)
email: sales@luath.co.uk
Website: www.luath.co.uk